THE ANGEL WHO LOST HER WINGS

Bahareh Amidi

The Angel Who Lost Her Wings

Baharah

Copyright © 2022 Bahareh Amidi. All Rights Reserved.

ISBN 978-0-9974573-7-7

cover and interior illustrations by
    Sara Nikforouz

email: connect@bahareh.com
facebook.com/Bahareh.Amidi
twitter.com/BaharehAmidi
youtube.com/baharehLIVE
instagram.com/bahareh_poetess
www.Bahareh.com

Listen to
The Angel Who Lost Her Wings

One day I finally knew I was here.

Here and Now

Once upon a time there was an Angel.
An Angel who lost her wings.

She saw the birds flying in the sky

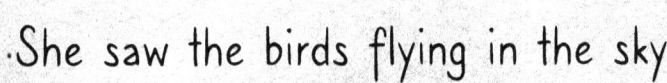

and the bees buzzing around

After years of sitting
She decided to walk again
and look for her wings
That is when she started
to fly wingless with heart

Listen to
The Angel Who Lost Her Wings

www.ingramcontent.com/pod-product-compliance
Lightning Source LLC
Chambersburg PA
CBHW040753020526
44118CB00042B/2936